Benjamin Schneider

Facebook Marketing

for entrepreneurs

Implementing a new project and making it successful is usually harder than you think. Nevertheless, I have a motto that accompanies me all my life: Giving up is not an option!
– **Ben Schneider**

Benjamin Schneider

Facebook Marketing for Entrepreneurs

This is how you increase your sales today by advertising on Facebook!

1st edition

Copyright © Benjamin Schneider

ISBN: 978-3-9819311-5-0

Creator and author:

Benjamin Schneider

Reinhartshofer Strasse 41

86845 Großaitingen

Photo Back Cover: Robert Hagstotz - http://hagaff-fotografie.de

For questions and suggestions:

Email: info@benschneider.biz
Web: http://www.benschneider.biz

Inhalt

Introduction by Dirk Kreuter

You send out mails? You make cold calls? You do cold visits in the field? You go to fairs? You exhibit at trade fairs and wait for visitors to come to you?

You can do all of the above, with more or less success. More likely: less success, since we are in the year 2017!

There is already the internet. By now, you can reach your customers and your potential target group online.

34 million people in Germany are online at least once every 28 days on Facebook.

You reach all consumers!

You believe that you do not reach the CEO of a DAX company on Facebook. You think seniors are not online? Could be.

But the children and relatives of the seniors - they are active on Facebook. Or the assistant of the board of directors, his daughter, his wife, who will tell what they have experienced there.

We are in the year 2017! Today you reach every subject online.

Why Facebook? On Facebook, you can accurately determine your target audience by gender, age, region and interests.

All of this is public on Facebook! For you, this means that every dollar that you spend on Facebook advertising will be used in a way that you would not be able to use with any other type of advertising budget.

This creates the opportunity, to all those who want to sell something, whether it be products, services or opinions, or even new employees, to achieve incredible success with a manageable advertising budget.

Just a few years ago, you would have had to spend six or seven figures in TV advertising to get the same results. In 2017 you can achieve the same results with only few tens of thousands of Euros.

Can anyone achieve that? No!

Only those who really have the expertise! If you do not know how it works, you will also burn your money on Facebook.

And for exactly this reason, this book that you are holding right now in your hands, is so immensely important and valuable.

This is your introduction into the new customer acquisition, into new sales regions, into more awareness and new employees.

I've known the author, Ben Schneider, for several years now.

He is an expert on the topic and not only tells how to do it. He also uses it for himself.

I wish you with this book many exciting insights, the discovery of a new world and of course "fat bucks!"

Dirk Kreuter is an entrepreneur, sales coach and speaker from Bochum. He is Coach of the Year, Speaker of the Year and in 2017 one of his companies was named one of the fastest growing companies in Germany. He invests seven figures per year in his online marketing business. He is the market leader in open seminars for sellers in Europe. Of course, you can also find him online on his website at http://dirkkreuter.com or on Facebook.

In a word

Welcome to my book about Facebook Marketing and especially about Facebook Advertising or as we will call it in this book, Facebook Ads.

To give you an idea, so you know who you are dealing with, I would like to introduce myself and explain why I'm going to address you informally in this book.

Let's start with the latter.

I will use informal language in this book because I think it will be easier for you as a reader to trust me while reading the book when I approach you like a friend, rather than a customer.

Among us internet entrepreneurs, there is no formal language and I apply this principle to most of my customers. This has nothing to do with lack of respect or excessive friendliness, but more with the fact that we do not have a rigid image or useless etiquette of each other.

What matters to us is the result and not how my counterpart looks like or speaks.

In the past you could engage in a lot of window dressing with a fine suit or an expensive watch. Today it does not work anymore, at least not in relation to the subject of this book.

Nowadays, almost everything is traceable on the internet. What matters is data and facts. Nice talk is out of place here.

Ben Schneider

In my online shop, I can see exactly if my customer came across an ad from Facebook or not. I can even understand how much money he spent on which ad.

We can generate an infinite number of clicks through Facebook, but since most people do not buy instantly, we can address these people again with additional retargeting ads.

We can target to people who have been visiting our online shop, put a product in the shopping cart, but finally did not buy.

That's exactly the power of Facebook ads, and I want to bring that power close to you in this book in order to boost your company's sales to the next level with the help of Facebook ads.

About the Author - Who is Ben Schneider?

My name is Ben Schneider.

I have been running my own online shop since 2013 and advise other online shops, as well as local companies in the field of online marketing.

My specialty here is Facebook Marketing with ads.

The interesting thing for you is that I do not only advise the companies classically, but I also create the ads and manage the advertising accounts of my customers.

This brought me in contact with a wide variety of industries and products.

I've sold everything from gold bullions and silver coins, to baby creams or trendy products in the USA. I have even placed ads for the distribution of silos for the agricultural sector.

One thing that you cannot learn in this book, is experience! The more often you do something, the better you will become. It's the same with Facebook ads.

It is important to me that I try to provide you with as much experience as possible in this book. But it is important that you not only read the book, but also implement what you have read. Only when you start to put your knowledge into practice, you will you get better with time.

Take this opportunity and learn from my mistakes and from my experience. The knowledge that you hold in your hands right now can generate you thousands of Euros in profits for your company in just a few weeks.

No, this is no exaggeration!

I've placed ads with 0,50 Euro per lead or over 1.000 Euros in sales with less than 20 Euro in advertising budget.

For one customer, we were able to send out 25 offers to interested parties with a total order volume of over 750.000 Euros within four weeks, by just using one single ad and less than 200 Euro in advertising budget.

This little excursion should give you an idea of the power and possibilities of Facebook ads.

At the moment, we are still in the beginning in Germany, because 95% of entrepreneurs are not familiar with it at all. That's why you should be prepared and not just in 2 years when everyone will do it and you overslept the next trend!

Take the time to read this book, take notes and read some chapters several times until you understand everything, because I would like to tell you one more thing: The less knowledge you have, the more money you will burn with your Facebook Ads.

Facebook ads are a weapon for any business owner, but only if you know how to use that weapon. Otherwise, you do not shoot like a sniper, but like a farmer who shoots with cannons at sparrows.

If you would like to receive more information about online marketing, E-commerce or Facebook Marketing after reading this book, I would recommend the following links of mine:

My YouTube channel: http://benschneider.biz/youtube

My podcast: http://benschneider.biz/podcast

Why Facebook Ads?

Before I explain the Why, I would like to clear up your exclusivity thought. This book is about Facebook ads and Facebook is really a great, if not the best, way to advertise currently online.

Nevertheless, there are also other advertising options, such as Google AdWords, newsletter advertising or search engine shopping ads, which are also good options.

So, for you as an entrepreneur or for your company, it's not about leaving everything else to one side, or even switching it off, and now thinking that all you have to do is Facebook advertising. It's about the fact that you introduce the advertising opportunity via Facebook ads into your marketing portfolio and thus create additional opportunities for you to win new customers and thus generate more sales.

Why should you start advertising on Facebook now?

In one sentence?

Because, it is the best way to reach your target audience right now, in my opinion.

Let's take a closer look at this statement.

When we think about a new marketing campaigns, apart from the ultimate goal of a sale, our goal is to reach the people we want to target with our advertising.

That's exactly what we can do better on Facebook than on any other platform.

On Facebook alone, I can already narrow down my target group by demographic information such as age, place of residence, gender or language.

But the better part is yet to come. Facebook knows not only how old we are and where we come from, but also what interests we have, which pages we like and what our current life situation looks like.

Sounds a bit scary from a user's point of view, right? Yes, I agree! ☺

But from the point of view of the entrepreneur who wants to run ads, nothing can be better than having a partner, in this case Facebook, who provides you with all the information about the people you want to reach. Because of this, you can choose exactly who you want to display your ad and to whom not.

The result is a lower advertising spend and higher conversion rates.

That alone would already be very good for us entrepreneurs. But I'll tell you straight away, what else you can do on Facebook and believe me, now it's getting really exciting.

Have you ever heard of a Custom Audience or Look-a-Like Audience? I do not want to anticipate too much now, as I will discuss this two target groups in later chapters in detail, but I would like to give you a little insight into the power of the target groups on Facebook.

You can create so-called Custom Audiences on Facebook. This means that you create your own personal target group.

Ben Schneider

For example, all people who visited your website or put something in the shopping cart.

In addition, you could create a target audience from anyone who has watched a video of you on Facebook, and thus turn on another ad that will be shown only to those who watched that one video on Facebook.

That would be the second opportunity to drastically reduce advertising spend.

Additionally, if I tell you that you can create so-called Look-a-like audiences on Facebook, where Facebook independently, for example, is looking for 1% of people, which behave similar to your custom audience, then you would probably call me crazy. ☺

I say yes, Facebook ads are a tool that you need to use for you and your business! It will not be any easier than it is now.

All of these audience choices have one goal, and that's what's important to you as an advertiser.

Your goal is to target exactly those people who are interested in your product or service.

Everyone, who you show your ad to, but who is not a potential customer means that you are burning your money.

In addition, you have a lot of analysis and tracking options on Facebook.

You can see which country and state your clicks are coming from. At what times people interacted with your ad. How many people actually clicked on your ad and bought. You can even see if it's a desktop, smartphone, tablet and Android or IOS user.

Yes, we are now all glassy people, but then at least we should try to be on the side where this information sharing can bring us an advantage.

Comparison:

Facebook ads vs. Google AdWords

There are currently two big players on the pay per click (PPC) ad market: Facebook and Google.

Especially through my videos on YouTube and my own e-commerce and online marketing podcast, I often receive the question which of the two makes the better form of advertising.

Short answer: There is no better form of advertising for me in this case, because those are two different systems, which should be used if possible both on their own.

Let's take a closer look at both types of advertising.

Google AdWords

The customer is searching!

With Google AdWords, I have no possibility to include images in my ad. I have an advertisement with two title lines, each consisting of a maximum of 30 characters, a description space for a maximum of 80 characters and the URL.

To whom my ad will be shown, can be decided during the creation by the selection of the keywords.

For example, I can choose "Facebook Expert", "Create Facebook Ads" and "Facebook Pro" as keywords for my ad.

If someone enters one of those three selected keywords in the search box in Google, my ad will appear above the organic search results.

I only have to pay, if someone clicks on my ad.

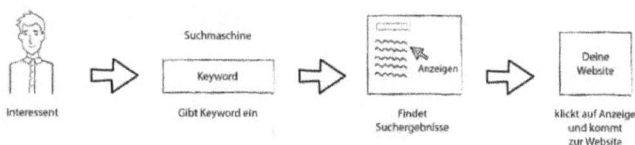

The advantage of this form of advertisement is clear, as it is the customer who is looking for something. The customer is looking for a solution to his problem, and by showing our ads on Google, we can get him to click on our website and present him with a solution to his problem.

Ben Schneider

The disadvantage with Google AdWords is that on the one hand I have almost no possibility to design my ads and on the other hand I'm not really able to define my customers.

I can only choose keywords, and anyone who enters this keyword will see my ad.

Facebook ads

I show the customer my offer! (whether he likes it or not).

Unlike Google, the potential customer does not search anything on Facebook. He may be simply on Facebook to check his messages or the status of his friends.

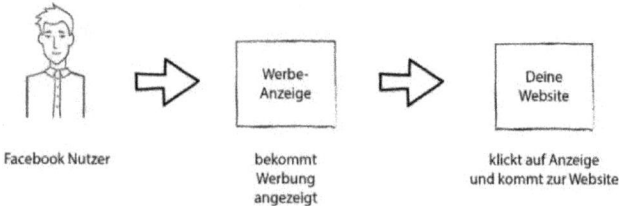

Facebook Nutzer — bekommt Werbung angezeigt — klickt auf Anzeige und kommt zur Website

Werbe-Anzeige — Deine Website

However, as he perfectly fits into the image of our selected target group, he/she gets our ad displayed.

Is he in the mood to see our ad?

- No idea ...

Does he have time to view our ad?

- No idea ...

Why should he click on our ad? - Because it is very interesting for him and can solve his problem!

Unlike Google, Facebook gives us the possibility to make our ad really beautiful and interesting.

We can insert a lot of text and smileys. In addition, we are free to work with pictures or videos. We can even create small landing pages behind an ad.

Ben Schneider

We also need all of these tools as the potential customer does not wait for our offer. He just gets it displayed.

But as the customer precisely fits in so well with our target group, this system still works. We sell something to our potential customers even if they have not been looking for it right now, but are basically interested in it.

As you see, there is no better or worse here. Of course, there are markets and industries where Google AdWords or even Facebook advertising might work better, but basically there is no either...or for me.

For me it's a combination of both. I'm trying to pick the best out of both platforms.

A little bonus tip that you will probably understand later:

You can combine both platforms easily. You get the searchers through your Google AdWords ads on your website and then show them Retargeting Ads on Facebook.

That's how you can combine both platforms, increasing your chances of turning prospects into customers.

Facebook Fan Page

Why a fan page is required?

In order to create ads on Facebook, you need technically speaking, a Facebook fan page for your company.

You have probably already created your own fan page for you or your company. Even if it does not have many likes so far, you can still use it to create ads.

Even if it would not be a technical requirement, you should have your own Fan Page for your business, since a private profile would not look legit for an advertisement.

Ben Schneider

How do I create a Facebook Fan Page?

To create your own Facebook fan page, first log in to Facebook with your private profile.

Then click on the arrow pointing down, in the upper right corner and select "Create page" in the menu.

Now you can choose between "Local Business or Location", "Company", "Organization or Institution", "Brand or Product", "Artist, Band or Public Person", "Entertainment", and "Good Purpose or Community".

In most cases it will probably be a "company, an organization or an institution". For example, if you are an online marketing expert then you can also select artist, band or public person here.

You can also change the type you have chosen here later, if you chose the wrong one here or if something else changes.

If you have decided on the kind of type, then click on the big picture.

Now you are asked for a category and a name for your business. Facebook wants to categorize the pages as structured as possible. Just choose what suits your page best.

If you click now on "Let's Go", then your new Facebook Fan Page will be created.

This page is of course empty right now. Neither profile picture, title picture nor any descriptions are available.

That's exactly what we need to create and do first.

Which graphics do I need?

In order to transform your Facebook fan page into something friendlier, we will start with the pictures.

You require two pictures for your basic setup.

A profile picture and a cover picture.

The profile picture should have a size of 160 x 160 pixels.

As profile picture you should choose the company logo or a picture with your face. If you have a great office building or if your company only sells one product, you can choose it as well.

The cover picture of your fan page should be 851 x 315 pixels.

For the cover picture, I prefer to not give you an advice on the design, because nowadays everything can be good or bad.

My only advice for you at this point, is that your cover picture should have a thematic reference to your business.

It is all about the corporate identity or, simply put, the recognition value of your brand for the customer.

Bonus tip:

Take a look at Fiverr (Fiverr.com) and enter "Facebook Design". There you can have your Facebook cover picture created by international designers for only 5 Euros.

Works great and you do not need to spend much time with it.

Which text content do I need?

You should add a short description to your Facebook Fan Page. The description must not exceed 155 characters and should briefly highlight the purpose of your company.

It is not about a long description, but rather 1-2 sentences.

In the menu item "Info" you also find the possibility to enter your website, your telephone number and your E-Mail address. I recommend to do so.

Whether you want to add more items, such as products, a menu or something else is up to you.

What we definitely need is an imprint! Also, on Facebook you are obliged to create an imprint.

Fortunately, Facebook has created its own menu item here. This is called "Imprint" and there you can copy the imprint of your website.

In addition, you can also set a link to your privacy agreements in the menu item "Privacy Policy".

I am not a lawyer and therefore I cannot give you legal advice, but you should insert an imprint and the link to your privacy policy in any case on Facebook.

Facebook Business Manager

Why do I need the Business Manager?

You do not necessarily need the Business Manager. The Business Manager is a separate platform on Facebook, in order to manage ads and your fan pages easily and quickly.

Since I work exclusively with the Business Manager for ads, I would also advise you to do so, since this tool is now very well developed and in my opinion, makes your daily work easier with Facebook ads.

When should I skip the Business Manager?

If you say that you'd rather stay in your familiar Facebook interface, then you can skip the Business Manager, or if you only have a page and an ad account, and you're the only person working with it.

In this case, you do not necessarily need the Business Manager, however, I would still use it in your place.

For whom is the business manager designed for?

The Business Manager is intended for those who either manage multiple fan pages and advertising accounts or work with multiple employees or agencies or service providers for Facebook marketing (advertising or social media content marketing).

Ben Schneider

For example, if you would like me to create and maintain your ads for your company, then you can invite me to your Business Manager as an "advertiser" and then I would get access to the areas I need. You do not need to provide any credentials or any insight to your private profile or messages.

Within the Business Manager you have a very good overview of all your fan pages and the various ad accounts in which the ads are running. There you can get all the complete insights into all statistics of the ads and page interactions.

How do I set up the Business Manager?

The setup of the Business Manager is really easy, because Facebook guides you through the steps.

You can log in under:

https://business.facebook.com.

Then you link your fan page with your business account and create an advertising account. For this advertising account, you will need to add a form of payment such as PayPal or a credit card.

Afterwards you can add more people, like yourself, your co-workers, or an external one, like me.

You should complete all your company settings so that your tax information, etc. are all properly filled.

After finishing this book, you can start publishing your ads.

You can create your pixel code there and upload your product catalog.

In the future, you will find all of your business activities in your business manager on Facebook, enabling you to separate the private from the business activities.

Ben Schneider

Facebook Ads

5 Typical beginner's mistakes at a glance

Before I explain them to you, I'd like to show you some of the typical mistakes beginners make on a regular basis and wonder why they burn their money on Facebook.

1. "Boost Post" - Button:

Facebook makes it easy for beginners to advertise with Facebook ads. If you have published a new post for your fan page, you will immediately find the "boost post" button under this post. We, who have more experience with Facebook ads hate this button because it encourages beginners to burn their money.

Why is that?

Very easy! If you click this button, you do not have the same options as when creating an ad through the Ads Manager. For example, you cannot set a manual bid for your actions using the "Boost Post" button. That would not be such a problem, as this is usually left to "automatic", but the main point here is that you cannot narrow down your target group as good as in the Ads Manager and that's exactly what it is all about on Facebook!

If you show your post to people to whom it is not relevant, you could also just throw the money out of the window.

Conclusion: Never use the "Boost Post" button on Facebook, and always create your own ads in the Ads Manager. There you also have the option to use an existing post in the last step of creating the ad, so you do not have to create it again.

You can find more about this in the next chapter, *Page Post or Dark Post advertisement.*

Ben Schneider

2. The Facebook pixel is neglected

Without any numbers, I do not know if the campaign is working or not!

Numbers, however, are only provided by the Facebook Pixel for my Facebook Ads. This means that if I do not include the Pixel on my website, I will not receive any numbers for my ad and I won't receive any numbers. And without numbers, I am unable to evaluate anything, which in the end does not give me the opportunity to see if my ad is working well or not.

Beginners often want to start quickly and easily. A common, but unfortunately totally wrong belief is:

"I start and if everything goes well, I can still install the Pixel later."

But this is complete bullshit because, as described above, you need facts to know if your ad is running well or not.

With the Facebook Pixel you know exactly where and how often people have clicked or bought something.

Conclusion: One of your first steps should be to integrate your Facebook Pixel into your website. Without the Pixel, you should not run an ad unless you have no website and only want reach for a local business.

How to install the Pixel and what exactly it does, you will learn later in the chapter **Conversion Pixel**.

3. The target group definition is missing

The most frequently made mistake on Facebook ads is forgetting or disregarding the target audience. By this, I mean to which persons the ad will be shown to.

As I already wrote, Facebook is not comparable to Google AdWords. We are not waiting for people to look for our product. We rather just show it to anyone we think could be a potential buyer.

That's why Facebook ads are all about choosing your target group. I tell you exactly what to look for in the **Audience Definition section**, but for the moment, I'd like to let you know that the audience definition section is one of the core topics on Facebook ads.

You cannot oversee that or just skip it, because you'll burn your money. You always have to narrow down your target audience as precise as possible, because that's the only way you can reach people to whom your product or service is relevant or interesting. This enormously increases your chances of selling something.

Conclusion: Make sure to spend time on the definition of your target group, otherwise you will burn your money.

Ben Schneider

4. An advertisement is enough

Beginners do not even come up with the idea to create multiple ads for the same target group. However, none of us knows what the target group will best respond to.

That's why you usually create multiple ads for a campaign goal. These are then tested for a few days against each other and then you can tell which of the ads works best.

The worse ones are turned off and for the best one, ideally you increase the budget.

Conclusion: Always create several ads for a campaign goal, because only by doing this you can find out which ad delivers the best results to your target audience.

5. Too much budget at the start

It doesn't make any sense at the beginning to start with a budget of 50 or 100 Euros per day.

It is much more important to test what works and what does not.

That's why I start every ad set with 5 Euros and then after about a week I'll see which ad has performed well and which did not.

The worst performing ad will be shut down and the good ones can keep running with an increased budget.

Try to increase your budget gradually. Only because your ad with 5 Euros works well, does not automatically mean that it will run equally good with 50 Euros per day.

The less money you spend, the harder Facebook works to deliver good results, but of course it also limits your reach.

Conclusion: Always start ads with 5 or 10 Euros per day and then analyze them after a few days. The good performing ads can be kept running and the budget can be increased by 50%, while the bad performing ads should be turned off.

Page Post or Dark Post advertisement?

Before I show you how to advertise on Facebook, I want to give you some basic knowledge on the way. When dealing with Facebook Ads, it is in my opinion quite clear that you will pay for missing knowledge.

The less knowledge you have, the more you will pay.

If you create a post on your Facebook fan page, then you have the option to click on "Boost Post" and to create an ad with just a few clicks.

However, I would not recommend that, as stated above, since you have limited options and therefore the chance to burn your money.

Actually, it is better if you use the Ads Manager for this. How it works, I'll tell you later.

If you want to promote this post, then this post is visible for anyone visiting your fan page.

We call this "Page post".

Now let's take a closer at the post type called "Dark Post".

A dark post is a post that can only be seen by a selected target audience. You can create dark posts through the Ads Manager and then promote them.

Unlike the page post, a dark post is not published on your Facebook fan page.

Dark Posts are only displayed to the audiences that you selected when creating your ad.

By the way, the Page Post and Dark Post are your ads. Text, picture, etc. form your ad on Facebook.

Both types of posts can be effective. Sometimes you would like to see a post even after the end of an ad cycle, if this ad is no longer profitable anymore, on the fan page.

For example, dark posts are displayed in case of specific offers towards a specific target group. An example would be people who added a product to the shopping cart but did not proceed to the checkout process.

If I create an offer specifically for these people, I do not want the offer to be displayed to everyone on my fan page.

Another example of creating dark posts is split testing.

When I create an ad campaign, I usually create multiple images and test which image best suits the audience. You can see this from interactions with the ad, such as likes or comments.

After a few days, a winner (the picture with the most interactions) emerges. Once I know which image works best, I turn off all the others.

This could not be done with page posts, as you do not want to annoy your fans with five equal offers and different pictures at the same time.

You can see that it makes sense to select the respective post type for the right target group and display it to them.

Page Posts: Posts that should be visible to everyone before and after the ad cycle.

Dark Posts: Posts that should only be displayed to a specific target audience.

However, you can also turn Dark Posts into Page Posts at a later stage and post them on your page.

The goals of your ad

The first step in creating an advertising campaign on Facebook is to choose a campaign objective.

In this step, you'll tell Facebook what your ad campaign target is.

To understand this step, you need to know that Facebook has developed an algorithm for displaying the ads on Facebook.

Facebook knows exactly which people, for example, like to click on an ad, or that are more likely to buy or which of them are likely to give likes to fan pages.

Based on this information, Facebook optimizes your advertising campaign with the goal that you set in the campaign objective. For instance, show the ad to people that are most likely to buy our product/service.

The algorithm works even better when sales are generated specifically for your ad.

At the beginning, Facebook will probably orient itself towards ads that have been shown so far.

However, once sales are generated through your ad, Facebook can optimize the ads even better and bring you more targeted potential customers.

I suspect that you need at least 50 sales, in order to optimize your Facebook Ads and to display the ads to an even better target group.

Therefore, it could make sense to run an ad little longer once it generates sales, as there is a possibility that the cost per sale will decrease as the number of sales increases.

Facebook is constantly optimizing its own website, but I'm taking the risk to list all the points here. There may be more or fewer campaign objectives at the moment you hold this book in your hands, but Facebook is in a process of continuous optimization, which leads to a permanent change of its interface.

Currently, you can choose from one out of eleven campaign objectives which are categorized in three campaign categories.

- Awareness
    - Brand Awareness
    - Reach
- Consideration
    - Traffic
    - Engagement
    - App installs
    - Video Views
    - Lead Generation
    - Messages
- Conversion
    - Conversions
    - Catalog Sales
    - Store visits

When selecting the campaign objective, not only does the objective change itself, but different campaign objectives also result in different ads or different buttons and setting options.

With a lead generation ad, the user can immediately share his data with you on Facebook.

Via additional services, such as Zapier or Leadsbridge, you can automatically integrate your leads into your E-Mail marketing software.

For example, if you're running a campaign with the objective product sales, your sales will be tracked through a different Pixel event than, let's say, a click campaign.

This distinction is important, so that you have correct data for the analysis later on.

That's why you should think carefully about the objective of your ad campaign.

Currently, it is even possible on Facebook, to start a conversion campaign by optimizing for link clicks and afterwards, after having received sufficient sales, Facebook can optimize the same campaign for conversions (= Sales) without your intervention.

By optimization of the campaign we refer not to the ad itself, but rather the delivery of the ads towards the respective target group.

Ben Schneider

Distinction:

Ad campaign, Ad group and Ad

In this chapter, I would like to explain something as vividly as possible to you, which I, for a long time as a beginner, did not understand when starting. The principle of how ads are structured on Facebook.

I've been creating ads for some time and had with some of them quite a success back then. Nevertheless, I did not really understand how the principle of advertising campaigns on Facebook is structured and what the individual subdivisions are for.

For your benefit, I eventually understood it and therefore I can pass this knowledge to you today. As a result, you do not have to invest a lot of money in Facebook advertising, as I did, to acquire that knowledge.

Once you've logged into your Business Manager and clicked on your Ads Manager, you'll see an overview of your ad campaigns.

You will now see, apart from your account overview, three tabs.

- Campaigns
- Ad sets
- Ads

All three are related but are responsible for different parts.

In the end, it all comes down to the ad, but before I start explaining the whole thing, I want you to imagine these small Russian wooden dolls, which are hidden in each other. You can open every wooden doll and a smaller one comes out. The same is true with Facebook ad campaigns, ad sets and ads.

By the way, these dolls are called "matryoshka".

When we create our advertising on Facebook, we go through all three areas.

At the beginning we configure our ad campaign. This is the first window when we create our advertising.

Here, we select the campaign objective (traffic, conversion, etc.) and give our ad campaign a name.

TIP: When naming, be sure to describe your campaign briefly but in detail, so when having 50 campaigns, you'll immediately see what the campaign it is about without having to search.

Example naming campaign:

Conversions - Facebook Course – Abandoned Shopping Cart

Later, in your Ads Manager, you will see campaign data in the Account Overview. But beware, all the data is included in here! Normally, if you do it well, you'll be creating multiple ad sets and more ads, so you will not get detailed knowledge from that data for analysis.

It does not help your analysis and optimization if you know that your ad campaign has generated 50 sales. You need to know which ad and which ad set generated those sales.

And here we come to the next tab, the Ad Sets.

In the second window, when you create a new ad, you get to the information that will be displayed later in the Ad sets section.

You define here your target group and where, when and how your ad will be displayed later.

This can include following: How old should the people be who see your ad, where do they live or where are they currently located, what interests do they have and much more.

You can also choose the ad budget for your ads, as well as where and when it should be displayed.

You can choose to display your ad only to Android users, only on the desktop, or only on Instagram, and so on.

It's important to understand that when testing different audiences, you're ultimately creating different ad groups, all in the same ad campaign.

So, an ad campaign can contain multiple ad sets. In addition, it is important to know that you can also set your own budget for each ad set. Not for every ad campaign, not for every ad, but for every ad set.

If we have defined our target group etc., then we go to the next step in the creation of our ad and reach the third tab in the overview, the ad.

The ad is what users will see later, so our creative. Here we define, on the one hand, via which Facebook fan page our ad should be displayed on the other hand, how it should look like.

Here, you can choose whether the ad should be a single image, video, canvas, carousel, and many more, and what text the ad should include.

You can also attach a parameter to your URL so you can track your visitors or customers even better, for example through Google Analytics.

Again, it's important to understand that you can create multiple ads in an ad set.

This is done, to test which image works best for a target audience.

I usually create five pictures for this and observe for a week which of the pictures gets the best reaction among the target group. I then continue to let this picture run and turn the other ones off.

Now you should have a good overview, so we can continue with the next chapters.

If you are not sure yet, or if you have not quite understood, then take another ten minutes and read this chapter again.

If necessary, take notes as well.

It is very important to me that you understand the whole principle I just explained. Simply, because you should not invest your money in something what you do not understand or where you still have a lot of questions.

Basic Marketing knowledge for advertisements

Before I explain to you step-by-step how to create an ad on Facebook, I'll just have to teach you some basics about marketing and sales.

Of course, this chapter may be boring or nothing new to you, but naturally there are many people who have bought this book and are not sales professionals.

My goal is to make it possible for you, through this book and my knowledge, to advertise on Facebook, which will give you or your company more sales and, of course, more profit.

I just have to teach you some basics, because without this knowledge about sales, you can save some money while creating your ads and lower your advertising budget.

In the following paragraphs, I will tell you which kind of sales methods can be used and integrated while creating a text, the headline, your pictures or videos in your ad, in order to get the user to click on your link or make them to give you their email address or even buy a product from you.

Please do not forget that the user on Facebook is not looking for our product. Rather, we just show him something that might suit him and thus a sale might be something that he is not prepared for at that moment.

Difficult task, but still possible! ;-)

Curiosity

Since the Facebook user certainly did not wait for our ad to show up, we must be able to get his attention. We may also get his attention for a short time while using a completely yellow picture, but he would just think, "oh, a yellow picture" and would keep scrolling down the feed.

That's why we have to be more creative. We have to think about which image would attract our customer and make him curious.

We need a TIMELINE BREAK with our ad. The user must interrupt his scrolling delusion and stop at our ad.

We can only do that if we attract his attention and arouse his curiosity.

Try to put yourself in the shoes of your customer when creating your image! What would he like to see? What could really interest him?

Honestly, most of my clients have been running ads on Facebook and using a product image for their ad.

Would a bottle of car polish cause you excitement and curiosity? No way!

However, what would be much cooler is a video that shows a totally dirty and scratched car and after polishing your car with it, leaving an almost new car behind.

Do you recognize the difference?

Boring pictures and ads are created by those who have no idea. There is enough of that, you do not have to join this "club".

Be creative and test different images for your target audience.

I guarantee you that if you create five images that are different but somewhat similar, you will still have a picture that is much better than the others.

I've been talking all the time about pictures and videos, but of course we have other ways to make Facebook users in our audience more curious.

We start with the description text above.

Description text

Do not start writing any poems here, but use bullet points or very short sentences instead.

Write in the first line something that attracts the attention of users. In the other lines you add various advantages of your product.

What advantages do I have if I buy this product?

Use smileys! Emoticons make your post much friendlier and attract more attention.

Attention! When creating your descriptive text, always pay attention to how it looks like on the mobile version. A preview you can be seen when creating your ad.

Most of the traffic that you will receive on Facebook is mobile. That's why it's very important that your ad on mobile devices, like smartphones or tablets, looks good and legit.

If you do not pay attention, your ad may look good on the computer, but on mobile devices you'll have ugly line breaks in the description.

Headline

Under your picture or video, you have the opportunity to place a headline. This headline is an integral part of any good ad. In this headline you should create curiosity for the user in few but concise words.

Example:

"How I converted 49,76€ into 2.168€ in Sales with Facebook!"

Or

"This is how I lost 20 kg of fat in less than 10 weeks!"

You should not promote any lies when creating your ads and headlines, but you must do everything to attract the user's curiosity. Only if he clicks, then you have the opportunity to convince him of your product.

It also does not help you if you boost your headline with something that you cannot deliver when reaching your landing page or online store.

You would have a great CTR (Click Through Rate), but at the end still no sales.

Just pick a headline that will spark your target audience's interest and fits thematically to your product.

A few more tips for designing your headline.

- choose your headline as short as possible
- use numbers
- use terms such as "new", "only", "free", "immediate", "special", "guaranteed", "exclusive", "fast", "limited", "secure"

Urgency

You absolutely have to buy right now!

Urgency is an integral part of every ad. If you are not short on deals, then your customer has no reason to buy right now. He must be afraid that this offer will soon be unavailable to him and that he will make a big mistake when not buying immediately.

Why?

Very easy. If you do not give your prospect an incentive to buy right now, then he will not. He may think, "Oh, I'll do that tonight or the next days," and then your potential customer is gone. For tonight he already has other things in mind and tomorrow he has forgotten your offer anyway.

While you can follow up on the phone or create online retargeting ads, in the end, it will be very difficult to make the prospective customer a paying customer because he no longer focuses on your offer.

When he sees your offer for the first time, it is something new he will deal with. It means that you must give everything in order to close the deal.

All the benefits must be put on the table and all doubts of the customer must be cleared aside.

And now to the important point.

You have to create scarcity for the offer! The message must be very clear:

"Customer, buy now or you miss the offer of your life"

"Only today", "There are only 3 places left", "Attention, this offer is only valid for a short time!"

You should use phrases like these or similar ones to indicate the scarcity of your offer.

Attention! Only honest scarcity is legitimate!

If you sell an e-book that you can sell and download 5 or 5,000,000 times, then you should not state "only 5 pieces available".

That would be dishonest and you should not do that!

Instead, start an action and make it clear in the ad that your E-book is now available for 9.99 Euros instead of 29.99 Euros, only this week.

By doing this kind of approach, it is also important that the price then increases the week after, otherwise your scarcity offer would not be honest.

By using urgency for the offer, we want to see a move from the prospective. If he clicks away, that's okay, then we'll try again via a retargeting ad, but a certain percentage will be triggered to act immediately and buy, and that's exactly what we aim for.

Benefits instead of features

One of the most important chapters in Sales!

We buy a benefit, not a feature!

What do you mean with that?

We do not buy a product because of its purpose, but we buy a product because it gives us a result that we would like to have.

Let's use some examples.

Do you want to have curly hair as a woman, or do you just buy a curling iron because it's so fun to wrap your hair?

Do you buy a ticket for a seminar because you like to spend your weekend in a hall with many other people, or because you will get the knowledge to be able to generate more sales?

Do you buy a new video camera, because you want a device with 20 megapixels and HD or because you want to create cool videos?

We do not buy features, but results.

A true story on the subject:

I was looking for a terminal server so that I and my employees, no matter where we are in the world, could access our programs and not be geographically bound.

Then I talked to an employee of a server company and he told me that package 1 had the CPU and X memory and X

Ben Schneider

hard disk capacity and package 2 this, and package 3 that, but not this feature and so much memory and blah blah.

I'm friendly and let him talk out, but when he was done, I said to him, "That's great to hear, but I'm an entrepreneur, not a server technician. I want to do it with XYZ and that should all happen in fast speed. My data should be secure and my employees should have access. I do not care if the server has or needs 3 RAM more or less, please recommend the package I need for my needs. "

One minute later we had a solution.

We do not buy features! I do not care what's in this box in any data center. I want the result and the resulting benefit!

Although you may not be able to imagine it at the moment, but that's the way it works with any product.

You do not want to eat! You want to be full! The full belly is what you want.

You do not want fish in the water. You want the time when you sit with your daughter in front of it and watch the fish with her.

You do not want any money in your bank account! You want the freedom that gives you the money!

Now pick two or three products out of your product range and think about what the customer really wants when he buys this product.

Even if you think at first sight, that you cannot do that or cannot find an advantage, once you understand it, then you will come up with a lot of advantages for each of your product.

Only when you have understood that, it's worth turning to Facebook ads, because only then will you be able to get people to purchase from you.

If you have not heard anything about this topic so far, this chapter is likely to revolutionize your sales business and approach and bring you a sales storm. If you know how to sell the benefits rather than features, your chances of selling to any potential prospect suddenly skyrockets.

So always think about what the customer really wants with this product!

Does he need a remote control or does he want to skip the three meters from the couch to the TV so that he does not have to get up?

The power of numbers

You should work with numbers when creating your ads whenever possible. Numbers usually attract a lot of attention and thus make the Facebook user stop from scrolling to read the information more closely.

Here, of course, we are back at the aspect of curiosity and with numbers we can make the prospective customer curious, as numbers always raise somehow the attention.

When I tell you that we have already sold 12,384 pieces of a product, you automatically associate it with a good product if it sells so often.

Maybe only my marketing is very good and the product very bad, which is why I got back 10,000 as a return. Do you know that? No, because you associate with a large number something positive or something positive for you.

Numbers not only bring us the attention of the curious prospective customer, but they also help us to sell the product easier because the interested person gets a better understanding.

Use the largest possible numbers! But what do you do if you do not have big numbers to show?

Using numbers is fine, but if you post an ad where you state that you've sold a product 3 times, that's a number, that will not convince anyone.

That's why you should always find the largest possible numbers. For example, you could state following about your shop: "We've had over 10.000 customers worldwide so far."

Another option would be to mention the number of positive reviews you have "more than 18.273 satisfied customers".

Sometimes you have to be creative, but there is almost always a way that you can use for your ads.

Important to me is only one thing at this point: Don't lie! Do not create numbers that are not related to your business.

You are the expert!

Do you consider yourself an expert or do other people see you as an expert?

That's a big difference, but mainly it will decide whether people buy from you or not.

If you now think that you are running an online store and therefore need no expert status, I hope that I will be able to teach you a lesson in this section.

We buy from experts! But how is an expert defined? In fact, there is a lot of scope for own interpretations, which many "experts" also make use of.

Wikipedia describes an expert as "a person who has an above-average level of knowledge in one or more specialized subject, areas or skills."

Well, as already mentioned before... a lot of room for interpretation. ☺

Especially in the field of online marketing or more specifically in the "expert business", the opinion has emerged that you can call yourself an expert, as soon as you know more than the people who are just starting to deal with the area.

Honestly, my opinion is different!

For me, an expert is someone who has above-average knowledge in his field and should also bring a certain amount of experience within his area.

Ben Schneider

This is an important aspect for me, as you cannot buy experience, even if experience has often been learned the hard way.

Thus, we would have clarified the expert status, but what does that have to do with your ad on Facebook?

As I mentioned at the beginning, people like to buy from experts. An expert has idea and experience. He knows what he is talking about and has already implemented the things he is teaching very often. What works for others will definitely work for me too – those are the customers' thoughts.

Would you have bought this book if I would give the impression with all my presence on the internet that I have no idea about Facebook ads?

Would you buy a product in an online shop if you are unsure if they even know what they are selling?

We all want to buy our products and services from companies that make us feel good.

Actually, that's also important in terms of pricing. Customers are happy to pay more when they feel better.

It is important for you that you position your company as number one contact on the market. Yourself and everyone in your company knows how the wind blows. You are the absolute experts on topic XYZ.

It is exactly this idea that you should reflect in your appearance. With the customer, with every e-mail, with your website and also with your ads.

If your ad is highly professional, but your online shop or website is cluttered, it will not do you any good. By the way, the reverse is true as well.

Include numbers in your ad to reinforce your expert status. It's called "social proof" in professional circles.

You can do this for example through customer reviews.

Convince other people who have never seen you or your company and never heard of you, that it might be interesting for them to take a closer look at your offer.

The simplest tips I can give you here are:

- Use professional pictures
- Pay attention to grammatical and spelling errors
- Give prospects the feeling that you are the best choice

Selling through pleasure or pain

There are only two ways you can sell a product or service. The two are called "pleasure" and "pain".

First, let's define what pleasure and pain mean.

Sale through pleasure

A sale through please is something beautiful. You sell ice cream by showing a picture of a happy woman sitting in a yard eating an ice cream. You think, "oh yes, I would like that now as well."

That's pleasure.

Sale through pain

You see on TV commercial where someone has bought a new car and caused an accident. Unfortunately, he has to pay the damage himself, because he had no full insurance.

You're thinking, "oh no, I should get a full insurance, to avoid that it happens to me as well."

That's pain.

Did you recognize the difference? Pleasure is a positive feeling. Pain is a negative feeling.

With a pleasure purchase, you always want to do something good. You want to have a nice time or make your life easier.

With a pain purchase, you always want to minimize your risk of loss. No one wants to have an insurance. But everyone wants to keep their risk as low as possible in case of damage.

When do we use which method?

Firstly, we should always try the pleasure method. Always show the benefits and the nice results of your product or service.

If that does not work, retargeting will allow you to address the same people who clicked on your page but did not buy it through the pain method.

Example:

We have advertised for a customer a foil for hay bales on Facebook. The foil is important for farmers, as the hay bales must breathe under the film and must not mold. If the hay is moldy, the feed for its animals is damaged for the farmer and that would mean enormous damage.

So, anyone who clicked on the ad but did not buy the product, will get another ad that leads to a blog post that explains to the customer how much damage he can do if he does not buy that foil and instead chooses a cheaper one.

It is undoubtedly much nicer to sell for pleasure and that should always be our first choice. Nonetheless, in the second attempt, you may also like to try the pain method to convince the customer of your product.

Some customers are actually grateful, and after the purchase, they write an e-mail in which they thank the company for alerting them regarding the risks.

But there are also industries in which the pleasure approach is futile. As already mentioned, no one wants to have insurance. You cannot sell insurance through pleasure, that does not work. You always sell insurance through pain.

Or take the example of a fire extinguisher. How do you want to sell a fire extinguisher over pleasure? The red color is so beautiful on the white wall or it fits so well with the curtains?

Here you do not need to think about a pleasure purchase because it simply does not exist.

Always think about whether you can trigger something positive with your product and if that is the case then try the pleasure variant.

Call to Action

"He sees where he has to click..." No, he does not!

For me, the point "call to action" has been for a long time confusing and meaningless. Why? Because everything that I know or can, is always natural to me. I thought for a long time that everyone can do what I can do and everybody sees the same what I see.

The truth is that people see nothing and react differently than you might think.

That's why we have to lead people. We really need to pick them up and tell them exactly where to click and if you're good, you'll tell them what they'll expect from this click and what they can do there.

As always, let's take an example:

You create a video ad on Facebook. In this video you say in the last sentence, "If you want the eBook for free now, then click on the button below this video. Then you come to a page where you can download your eBook for free. "

Now you've asked your prospect to act. You have told him what to do, increasing the likelihood that he will do what you expect him to do.

I know you might think that you're giving him a free eBook with infinite knowledge, and he must know where to click it and how to download it.

No, he does not know!

We have to tell people exactly what they should do and we should also tell them, what to expect.

People are not all that familiar with the Internet. The Internet is full of threats and everyone tells you that there is something at half price or even for free or how you can become a millionaire without any knowledge and without capital in 4 weeks.

Of course, people are scared then. That's why we have to urge them to act and give them clear instructions.

This does not just apply to your Facebook ads, but also to videos on your landing pages or similar sales pages.

Whenever you want your prospect to do something, you have to tell him.

Step by step instructions for creating an ad

Optimization target

Before we create the ad or select the target audience, it's all about what we want to achieve with our ad.

What is the goal of your ad?

Selecting the target is important because, on the one hand, the following functions are different when creating your ad campaign, and on the other hand, the delivery of Facebook itself is a bit different.

Facebook automatically optimizes the delivery of your ad with regards to your specified campaign goal.

Facebook is able to do that because they know how we behave. If our behavioral patterns tell them that we are likely to buy Product X, then we're also more likely to see an ad regarding Product X.

Everything that you can and should differentiate, I have already explained to you in detail in the chapter "The goals of your ad", so let's move on to the next chapter "Conversion Pixel".

Conversion pixel

The conversion pixel.

This is one of the most important chapters in this book. Not because of its content, but because of the topic!

Without conversion pixels, there is no retargeting of your website visitors.

If you do not use Retargeting ads on Facebook, then you are giving away a lot of money, because with retargeting you are addressing people who were already on your website and thus are no longer completely cold traffic.

Moreover, you need the pixel on your website to keep track of the leads, your sales and the value of your sales.

In short, Facebook ads without the installation of the Facebook Pixel make no sense when you promote something on a website!

That's why installing your Facebook Pixel installed on your website should always be one of your first actions.

You can find your pixel in the Business Manager under the menu item "Pixel". Alternatively, you can also find it, if you want to create for example a new conversion campaign, under the menu item "Ad set" under "Conversion". Here you can either select the respective event for your ad or, if you have not yet configured and installed a pixel, you have the possibility to do so.

I'll explain the quick version of how to install your Pixel. I do not want to save lines here, but this is the only way it works very well for beginners as well as for professionals.

You are looking for your system, such as WordPress, or your shop system, such as Magento, Shopify or Shopware, a suitable plugin.

If this plugin costs a few Euros, then please invest the money, I'll tell you why.

If you have the plugin installed, then all you have to do is enter your Facebook Pixel ID, click on Save and your installation and configuration is done!

You now have all events, such as "Website Visits", "Product added to Cart", "Initiated Checkout", "Purchase" and "Lead" etc. functionally installed.

If you worked without a plugin, you would have to install a separate pixel code with your own event "purchase" on every single page, such as the checkout page (page after the purchase).

If you simply install the HTML code of Facebook in your head area on your website, you have no events and cannot track the conversion values (only if the product catalog is linked).

IMPORTANT! Always check if your Facebook Pixel works properly!

You can do that for example with a free extension for the Chrome browser called "Pixel helper".

This might sound very profound to you and you may be thinking, *"Oh, I just want to test it out once, I do not need that now."*

But that's a mistake. You need all the data, otherwise you will not know how good or bad your test really is. How do you know if an ad is performing well, if you do not know how much revenue you made on this ad and how many sales it made?

Install your Facebook Pixel on your website before starting with your ads!

It is also important for you to know that you have one Facebook Pixel per ad account. You can install your Facebook Pixel on different websites.

Due to the help of the Facebook Pixel, you will not only be able to see how many leads, clicks, or sales your ad has generated for you, but you can also create custom audiences, and in turn, run retargeting campaigns.

Target group definition

The target group definition is more or less the most important part of creating your Facebook ad campaign.

A bad ad can work for the right audience, but a good ad shown to the wrong audience will never produce good results.

To make sure that you understand it completely, I will give you an example

If you're a convinced vegan, then you will not click on an ad with the slogan "Today's meat at a special price!", let alone buy something. No matter how good this ad is, because you're against meat. The ad can be as good as possible, you will never buy a piece of meat.

Well, I think that's clear now. ☺ It is absolutely important that you display your offer to the right target group.

Demographic selection

If you're just at the beginning, then you will start off with a campaign based on demographics. Of course, it can also be worthwhile later to select your target group according to demographic information.

In terms of demographic target group selection, we talk about defining our target audience with information that lets us choose Facebook. These can include for example the age, the place of residence or the language.

In addition, we can also select the areas of interest and employment of the future target group.

However, with Facebook we can go much deeper. We can categorize the target group according to their income or even according to religious orientation. Marital status and the child situation can also be selected.

There are other choices, but the best thing to do is if you click through Facebook on your own and check, as this list is so large that I could fill an entire book.

Nevertheless, I would like to give you an example.

Let's assume that you are a goldsmith who offers wedding ring courses and wants to promote them on Facebook.

For example, your target audience could be selected as following:

- Residency in Munich and 80 km radius.
- Language: German
- Age 21 – 50
- Marital status engaged
- Estimated monthly income over 2.000 euros net
- Interests: Everything related to weddings - dress, photographers, rings, music, etc.

If you choose this, then you can be sure that you will find a relevant audience for your offer. Of course, you could also differentiate between men and women, but personally I would not do that in this case, because I would first test it, which gender reacts better to the ad.

An important point that you should pay attention to, in any case is that you can also narrow down interests or target groups with the interest selection.

For example, you may say the person needs to be interested in a wedding dress, but also in a wedding photographer.

This interest-limiting option makes a lot of sense for your audience selection in most cases.

Another thing to keep in mind is that you can also exclude people with demographic information.

For example, you can say, that the person needs to be interested in a wedding dress as well as in a wedding photographer, but all those who are estimated to make more than 5.000 euros a month should be excluded.

Ben Schneider

You just have to click through and pick the right one for you. The best way to do so, is to use your customer avatar and look at the right data on Facebook.

Do not overdo this point too quickly, but invest a lot of time, because as mentioned in the beginning of this chapter, the best and greatest ad does not help you if you show them to the wrong target group.

If you've created a targeted audience that you think you'll need more often, you can save the audience and later use it again by clicking a button.

Custom Audience

If you already have data about your target group, then you can create your own target audience (= Custom Audience).

There are some ways on Facebook how to create a custom audience. You can, for instance, upload the E-Mail addresses of your target group to Facebook. Another way to create a custom audience is to use recent visitors to your website.

If you have installed the Facebook Pixel on your website, then anyone who visits your website will be tracked with this pixel. By doing so, Facebook finds those people again. If your website or even a single landing page was visited by a few hundred people, then it can make sense to create your own custom audience, since these people already know your product or service.

You can also be more specific when creating a custom audience by selecting that the user must have visited page A on your website, but not yet seen page B.

Simply explained, this means, for example, that the visitor could have added a product to the shopping cart in your online shop, but not yet purchased it.

In this case, you know exactly who you can address this abandoned shopping cart user with another ad.

These distinctions can be incredibly important later, because the more specific and accurate you can define your audience, the more accurate you can address them later, and the greater is the likelihood that they will use your offer.

Ben Schneider

Creating a custom audience from your website traffic always makes sense!

Meanwhile, Facebook has continued to improve and that's why there are even better and especially useful features, such as creating your own custom audience without having an own website.

All you need is a Facebook Fan Page.

I won't list all the options, because that would not help you at this point, but we will take a closer look at the most important ones.

You can see it yourself if you want to create a new Custom Audience and then click on "Interactions".

Here you find a list with video, lead form, full screen experience, Facebook page, Instagram business profile and events.

Bummer, now I've listed them all. ☺

It's about being able to create a target audience of people who have interacted with the ones mentioned above (fan page, events, etc.).

That's really useful.

If we take a closer look at the video area, there you can find more possibilities to limit it. For example, you can say that your custom audience should only include people who viewed a particular video more than 50%.

Why does that make sense?

If you want to sell a product to build an online store with your ad and this product is not the cheapest, then you need people who are interested in building the online store and have built trust in you.

Now, if you include all the video clicks, including those people who watched the video for just five seconds, then you might have many people in this group for whom your product is out of the question, or who still have too little faith in you.

That is just an example, but I hope you understood the basics of this idea.

Important to you, and this is one of the key messages of this book is that you understand that you need to narrow your target audience as closely as possible.

Only then will you reach the cheapest ads with the greatest revenue potential.

Let's look at the point Facebook pages, which also comes with a huge potential.

You see, Facebook ads are so exciting, you could easily write a whole book about it! ☺

Also in the section Facebook pages, you have the opportunity to use more choices.

Currently Facebook offers the following:
- Everyone who interacted with your page
- Everyone who visited your page

- People who interacted with a post or an ad
- People who have clicked a "Call to Action" button
- People who sent a message to your site
- People who saved your page or post

Why are these functions useful? Because they always work according to the same principle! Limit your target audience as much as possible!

If someone has sent you a message to your fan page, then we can assume that the person knows you and probably wants some advice from you.

This means that this person has confidence in you, and if someone trusts in someone else, the chance is far greater that the person will buy something, in comparison with someone who does not know you at all.

Many entrepreneurs give away an incredible amount of potential, simply because they do not use the lukewarm traffic that they built up over time.

Most people create ads, whether on Facebook or elsewhere, to bring people to your site.

However, very few people create further ads to persuade the people who were on the site but did not end up buying a product, and that's where the greatest potential lies!

The creation of Facebook ads is often a game with the custom audiences, but use the tools that Facebook provides you! Only if you spend a lot of time understanding this, you will be able to achieve good results in the long term.

Look-a-Like Audience

The Look-a-like audience could be seen as an extension of Custom Audience. In this case, you do not create a new target group of data yourself, but you rather give Facebook a finished target group and Facebook creates its own target group with people who are very similar to this target group.

Let's take an example:

You create a Custom Audience of all people who bought from you (using the checkout page as a benchmark). You will now create a Look-a-Like Audience.

Then, Facebook looks at the profiles or the interactions of your buyers, creates an average of them and looks for other profiles that have similar behavioral patterns.

Why? Because if Hans has bought from you and Thomas is similar to Hans and has the same interests, then the probability is relatively high that Thomas could also buy from you.

I think you have just discovered a WOW moment regarding Look-a-Like Audiences.

This tool is really the big deal! This is how you can turn a functioning target group into a new, extended target group.

It is important that you read the top sentence again. You are turning a FUNCTIONING audience into an extension.

Not from a target audience that would fit, could or should, but from a target audience that already has bought! That's a huge difference that can really bring you a lot of money for your business.

Unfortunately, I need to calm your euphoria a little bit now, because you need data to create a Look-a-Like audience.

Facebook can only look for people who behave similarly, if you were able to deliver them people (data), who have already behaved as desired.

In my opinion, Facebook forms an average of the respective behavioral patterns, so the more is always better here.

For instance, if you have had 3 sales, then you do not need to create Look-a-Like Audience, as it won't be able to create a decent average.

If you want to work with decent Look-a-Like Audiences, then you should remember the number 100.

You should have at least 100 visitors on one page or 100 buyers so that Facebook can start off.

As I said before, the more is always better, so if you have 500 or 1000 sales, your Look-a-Like Audience will certainly be even more accurate than with 100 sales. Anyway, I think you can start off with 100 for a Look-a-Like Audience.

Placement

You have different possibilities where your ad can be displayed on Facebook, Instagram and in the audience network.

Let's start with the question Mobile or Desktop?

The standard is "all devices". That means that your ad will be displayed on both mobile devices, such as smartphones and tablets, as well as on classic computers and laptops.

However, you also have the option to display your ad exclusively on mobile or desktop devices.

If you have included mobile devices, no matter if you chose only mobile or all devices (including desktop), then you can also decide whether to include or exclude Android or iOS.

This distinction can make a lot of sense when you sell operating system-specific products. In this way, an app which does not have an iOS version, does not have to be displayed to Apple users. Also, if you're holding your Apple iPhone in your hand, you do not need to display an ad for a bag of the latest Samsung Galaxy.

It's always about narrowing down the target audience as much as possible, and with these options you can do that very well.

When does it make sense to include or exclude desktop or mobile devices?

Again, the example of an app is a very good one. To promote an app via the desktop PC is not as meaningful as promoting it directly via the smartphone.

Often, I also create different ads for mobile and desktop versions, because the form of presentation differs slightly and I try to target the campaign more precisely and thus get more success.

Furthermore, we have placement options on the various platforms and I would like to go through these with you individually.

Facebook

Feeds

Facebook Feeds means that your ads will appear on the Facebook News Feed. This is the area where you can see all the normal pictures and videos of your friends on Facebook.

Many times, I show my ads exclusively here. You can disable this option, but only if you want to advertise exclusively on Instagram.

There is one more exception. The Messenger messages, but it goes without saying that a messenger ad cannot appear on the newsfeed.

Instant Articles

Instant Articles only work on mobile devices and only in conjunction with the Mobile News Feed.

Instant Articles are pages that are directly downloaded from Facebook. These are mainly used for news posts and have very fast loading times on mobile devices.

Since these are articles from mostly large publishers, you have the opportunity, for example, to reach National Geographic readers with your ad here.

Like always, you have to test and see whether your ads are working in instant articles.

In-stream video

You probably already know this from YouTube if an ad is shown in front of, or in the video. Similar to Facebook, but here you can only use In-Stream ads with the campaign goal "Video Views" and your In-Stream promotional video should not be longer than 15 seconds.

This option is probably out of the question for most of your ads, but it may be worth a try for some action.

Right column

I guess there is not too much to explain about it. If this option is selected, then you will find your ad in the right column on Facebook.

I recommend this option only if your image alone is clear enough to help the user understand your ad or become curious. Do you need a few lines as an explanation or even a video, then the right column as ad placement is in my experience not interesting.

Suggested videos

This is only possible with the campaign objective "Video Views". Here, your video will appear after a video has been played, if there are more matching videos proposed, they will appear under the actual video.

Instagram

If you want to advertise on Instagram, it is important for you to know that the audience on Instagram is completely different than on Facebook.

You can and should create your own graphics and video formats for Instagram, because everything is in square format. We must give the user the best possible experience with our ad.

Instagram has two placement options. On the one hand, on the Instagram News Feed and on the other on the Instagram Stories.

In my experience, advertising within stories tends to be a bit worse than newsfeed. Nevertheless, you should try it yourself, as always, because your target audience can act completely different from mine.

Important, but obviously clear is that your advertising is of course only played on mobile devices because Instagram does not exist for the computer. You can view Instagram via the browser, but you have a very limited functionality and no ads.

Ben Schneider

Audience Network

If you want to advertise via the audience network, then you do not know exactly where this ad will be displayed since the ads will be included with external partners.

Your ad could then be seen, for example, as a small banner on apps like Angry Birds, or websites like the Bild newspaper.

Again, your image, your banner, should be meaningful enough for these ads to work, as there is no text here. If you have a video, that too can work well if you target "Video Views."

Messenger

You can post ad messages directly into people's messenger. That sounds cool at first, but only with people who have already written you a message on your fan page.

Nevertheless, that's still pretty cool, since you're reaching people directly, almost like a chat bot. This method is often much more efficient than traditional ads because it's warm traffic.

But as I said, this is only possible with people who have already exchanged messages with your page.

I have listed now all different placement options which are currently available. As already mentioned, I personally tend to select the Facebook Newsfeed most often as my ad option. However, you cannot generalize it, because other placement options can work also very well.

You just have to try it. Create multiple ad groups and always choose a different ad option.

After a week, you'll see which one has the best numbers (CTR, clicks, CPM, etc.). The best placements, keep them running, while turn the worst ones off.

Budget & Schedule

Advertising budget

You can choose on Facebook if you want to work with a daily or a lifetime budget. What that means in detail, I will explain to you immediately. But first I want to state a wrong belief.

"You need a lot of money to advertise."

This statement is actually no longer true. Of course, you require a certain budget, as you probably need to test different ads and maybe not every ad brings immediate success. The bottom line is, however, that you can turn start Facebook advertising with one Euro!

That means that you can create your own ad campaign per day starting with one Euro and show it to the world out there.

Of course, you won't reach many people with this one Euro (I estimate about 100), but even so, sales can result.

I always test a Facebook ad at the beginning, whether it's for myself or for my clients, at 5 Euros per day.

I do that to burn as little money as possible and thus to find out which ad works best. Naturally, I create several ads and I use five Euro as daily budget for each ad, but that's the way I burn the least money.

Only once I have a clear winner, I increase the budget and turn off the bad performing ads.

My recommendation is: start with five Euros a day and if the ad works, then increase the budget.

If it does not work with five Euros a day, then it will not work with 50 or 500 Euros per day either.

Daily Budget

If you want to create an ad with unlimited duration, then you are working with a daily budget. For example, you pay 5 Euros a day and Facebook delivers your ad throughout the day until the ad budget is exhausted.

You therefore have absolute cost control.

The daily budget option lets you work with a schedule. You can choose when to start the ad and when to stop it.

The lifetime budget requires you to work with a schedule because you need to set the lifetime for your budget.

More in the next paragraph.

Lifetime Budget

If you want to work with a lifetime budget, then your ad is defined for a fixed period, for example from 01.04.2019 to 01.06.2019. For this period, you enter your budget, for example, 350 Euros.

In this case, you also have full cost control, because you know exactly, the ad will cost you during this period 350

Euros and on 01.06.2019, this will be automatically turned off.

With lifetime budget, I would only work if you know for sure that this ad should be turned off at a certain date, for example, when you advertise an event.

Schedule

In this section, you can choose the times at which your ad should be delivered. For example, if you choose from 1pm to 3pm, your ad will only show on Facebook during that time of the day.

But before you think, "great, then I'll deactivate it at night," you should ask yourself if that really makes sense.

Is your audience really inactive at night or willing to like your site or buy your product?

My opinion is that anyone who sees the ad on Facebook is also able to realize an action, in this case, a purchase.

When do time schedules make sense?

If you have a temporary offer.

For example, if you run a live shopping offer every day from 7 - 8 pm in your online shop, then you should only advertise in this period or shortly before.

The background is that your ad should bring people directly to your page, where they can immediately participate in your live shopping.

Therefore, it does not make any sense to show the ad at 9 pm, because your live shopping is over by then and tomorrow they have forgotten it anyway.

If I do not pursue a time-limited objective, then I leave the ads on automatic schedule, because I even had at night at 2 am Facebook sales, which I would not have had without showing that ad.

Bid Value

We have the option on Facebook to enter a bid value or not.

For instance, how much is a link-click worth to me?

If you leave this option as automatic, then Facebook categorizes you based on the parameters of your ad and the competitive situation.

If you manually set your bidding path and we assume that you would choose it very high (5 Euros per click), Facebook will prefer your ad over other ads.

This can work well especially for a very small and well targeted audience. Of course, what you should always keep in mind is the cost-benefit calculation. It does not make any sense to pay high click prices if I have a very low margin or low-price products.

If you are still at the beginning, I would recommend that you leave the bid value on automatic. Professionals can try this option, but beginners can quickly burn more money than they want to.

Ad

Image ad or video ad?

One of the questions my viewers often ask me on YouTube or my podcast is:

"Ben, what's better for my Facebook ad, a picture or a video?"

The clear answer that no one likes to hear is:

"It depends on your objective!"

Sucks, I know, but let's take a closer look.

Generally speaking, I can already tell you: A video is usually better for your ad. However, that does not mean that a picture cannot work as well or even better.

Why do videos usually work better on Facebook?

Our social media world is very fast paced and above all entertaining. Every day we see thousands of pictures and quickly scroll over them without really looking at them. Our brain scans an image on Facebook in fractions of a second and decides whether it is relevant for us or not. If it decides no, we keep on scrolling immediately.

When displaying a video, that is not so easy, since we do not only see the first picture or even the first 1 - 3 seconds. Based on this information, our brain decides whether it be relevant to us or not.

In comparison to a picture, a video still has the surprising factor of not knowing whether any relevant information is hidden in the video for us. That's why we often tend to watch videos just to find out if there's something interesting in terms of content for us.

Obviously, it happens very often that we then turn off the video after a few seconds and afterwards realize that we wasted 2 minutes pointlessly on Facebook with a video.

Nevertheless, that does not change the fact that we are curious and like to be entertained. It just works much better with a video than with a picture.

Because a lot of things happen in a video, the interaction rate is also much better than with normal pictures. For pictures, this usually works only if you immediately recognize at first glance what it is about and understand the message or the joke behind it.

Your video should not be longer than a minute. As I mentioned, while we filter all relevant information from the video, we are no longer willing to pay for it with our precious time.

Let's put the facts on the table. We are impatient and want everything for free as fast as possible. Sad but true.

If you create a great video now, that lasts around 8 minutes, you will have a maximum of 2% of people who will watch your video until the end. If you create a great video, which is about a minute long, then maybe you will have 30% of people watching it until the end.

Ben Schneider

And if you think now, "what, only 30% for a very great video? That's too little?! ", then you should get used to low percentages on the Internet. Few people perform the desired actions as you would like them to do. Most people scroll over your offer, quickly click away, or simply do not take advantage of your offer.

You could give away knowledge today that would allow someone else to make millions of dollars a year, and still very few would take advantage of your knowledge, even though it would be free.

The people are like that. In my opinion this is a result of overstimulation. People are interested in everything and nothing. On the one hand, the offer is so large that there are 1000 offers that tell you how to become a millionaire step by step. If you have registered as someone who is interested in these kind of offers, then after the 20th sign up you will probably stop registering, as the offers has become so redundant.

However, don't worry about this kind of trend, as the good ones will always prevail against the bad ones in the long term. You just have to prove that your offer or your online shop is better than the competition and then eventually you will have the advantage on your side.

So, now we have immersed into psychology. Now let's have a look, when a picture and when a video should be used.

Basically, like with any other options, you must test them. I cannot give you a 100% correct answer in this book, as there is always room for exceptions, so test if necessary, only then will you really know what works better for you.

I have set the following rules for myself:

- If you want a lot of interactions (likes, shares, comments) then use a video.
- If you want to sell something that can be better viewed with a video than a picture, then use a video.
- If you want to build a lot of trust with your ad, then use a video.
- If your product does not need to be explained in depth, try a picture.

With these simple rules, I have done very well for myself and my customers so far.

I basically prefer to work with videos because they have a higher interaction rate, which means that the ads are usually cheaper than image ads and they also often achieve better results.

Display Text

Before we get straight to the text section of your ad, I'd like to let you know that you can preview the different types of devices on Facebook when designing your ad on the right side. Important for you are only the first two variants, desktop and mobile.

Desktop, is in my opinion only important if you plan to have your ads displayed only on the desktop. If this is not the case, then I would recommend that you always orientate yourself towards the mobile version when designing texts, such as headlines or descriptions.

The reason for this is that Facebook is mainly used by mobile users via the smartphone. The interaction rate is here the highest and unfortunately the attention span the lowest. However, your ad will be mostly displayed on the mobile version if you have not defined it yourself. Accordingly, it is important that your ad is best viewed on mobile versions.

That's why my recommendation is, to always open the mobile preview and then design your ad accordingly if you do not want to create a different version for each device (desktop, mobile).

However, if you want to do it very professionally, then you can create two different ads for mobile and desktop.

Title

The title is not displayed on Facebook, as one might assume, above all, and thus at the top, but rather below your image or your video.

If you have the mobile preview open, you will see in real-time what your title will look like in your ad. Make sure it fits in one line and is not too long.

It is important, that you create curiosity for the user with your title and/or advertise your offer as clearly as possible.

The Facebook user should be able to immediately recognize what your post is about or make him/her so curious that he/she looks at your text, image, or video.

Here are some things to keep in mind:

- Awake the users' curiosity
- Be as precise as possible
- Work with smileys
- Work with numbers

- Work with words like "offer", "free", "only today", "discount", etc.
- Choose the title as short as possible

Text

The description text of your ad is a very important part that is often given too little attention by beginners.

Facebook is not an ad network, and few Facebook users are able to differentiate ads from everyday posts.

Advertising is of course something bad and therefore no one wants to click on an ad, comment or even share.

Therefore, we have to make sure that our advertisement looks as generic as possible, as if a normal Facebook user had created a post.

In my opinion, it is very important that you work with smileys. I do not want to make a recommendation, but type into Google "Facebook Smileys" and then you take the first page that is displayed. ☺

I usually do not work with long texts, but with individual short sentences or keywords. I try to make the offer as clear as possible and show the advantages of the products, while creating the text of my ad.

In the mobile version, you have more lines available, as in the desktop variant. There, your text area is truncated and given a "... more" after six lines, while on the mobile you usually have nine lines available.

But you do not necessarily have to take advantage of these. Three benefits are usually sufficient, but you can also do your own tests by simply duplicating your ad and creating one with three benefits and one with five benefits. You can do that for 1-2 weeks and look if you can see a big difference in your numbers.

In addition, you should include a "Call to Action", so an action request into your text.

Possible examples of this are:

- Click on the button now.
- Share the video with your friends.
- Tag 2 friends who need to see this.
- Sign up now.
- Get your great offer now.

When creating your text, make sure that you make everything short, concise and clear. We have already learned that people do not have time to read. Your text must be very easy to scan by the user's brain. To make it as relevant as possible, you should include benefits.

Here's a quick summary of the most important data for your text:

- work with short sentences
- work with smileys
- arouse the curiosity of the user
- integrate a call to action
- include 3 - 5 benefits

Description of the news feed link

This section will appear under the title and above the displayed link below the image/video. For this part I always use a few smileys and 2 - 3 advantages of the offer. This simply helps the user to show how good this offer is and that he should not miss out on it.

Although you have some space here, you cannot work with paragraphs. Therefore, usually limit yourself to 1-2 lines.

Also make sure that you keep this text section as simple and clear as possible for the user.

Ben Schneider

Parameter

This part can be important for your tracking. If you want to create your own URLs with Google Analytics or in your online shop system, you can enter these additional parameters here.

By doing this, the inserted URL is always appended to the URL you included on Facebook. This usually looks like this: „?parameter=kampagnexyz".

ATTENTION!

If you work with parameters, then test the button of your ad immediately after completion, because this can also lead to problems. If your link leads to a non-existent page, then you're paying for an ad that does not work.

How to create an ad that goes viral

Here we go! If you can do that, you are the King!

Why? Because with an ad that goes viral, you get far more organic traffic than paid traffic through your ad.

Okay, let's start step by step.

What does it mean when we say that an ad goes "viral"?

This simply means that through many likes, comments, and frequent sharing, your ad reaches more and more people without the necessity to influence or even do anything about it.

You can think of it as a snowball rolling down the hill. It is getting bigger and faster, without your interference.

This leads to more and more traffic to your website and more likes, shares and comments on your ad, without the need to share it and without having to increase your budget.

Everything happens organically and from your point of view, automatically.

Ben Schneider

Of course, this sounds great and if you would be able to do that, that's even better. However, I have to tell you, that in reality, that happens very rarely.

Let's have a look at some of the topics that can make an ad go viral.

Animals

We all know them: the cat videos! Sweet, funny and attractive, without having to think about yourself. People love puppies or clumsy animals. With this you can land a viral hit.

Babies

People do not only love animals but also babies. Again, the same motto applies, the clumsier and sweeter, the more likely the user will interact with the video (like, share, comment).

Unbelievable things

"WOW, how does he do that?", "Oh, you see, is he suicidal or what?". If you think like that or similar, then you can be sure that this video has the potential to become an internet hit.

We want to show things that fascinate us also to other people. According to the motto: "Look at that, that's crazy!"

Subconsciously, we want to show this to someone in order to get the recognition that we have shown it to the other person. According to the motto: "Wow, thank you for sending me this video".

That's why we share such videos and put our opinion under the video.

News

Things that are completely new to us or seem unimaginable, also have the potential to go viral.

An example would be videos of self-driving cars, wireless security cameras or selfie drones.

The reason why we share these contributions is always the same, we want to be recognized for it, but of course we only share contributions where we think that we could receive this kind of desired recognition.

Ben Schneider

For this reason, the post needs to flash ourselves before we consider sharing it with our friends on Facebook.

I've given you four topics that offer great potential for a viral ad.

Now you have to try to combine that with your own product.

Posting a cat video, which gets 4 million views, does not help you a lot, since you are here to sell products.

If you are a little deeper in the subject, you could now create a plan to post a video with the goal of going viral, and then show to everyone who viewed the video, a retargeting campaign with the product that you are selling.

Great strategy, right?

Would that work?

No, it would not!

Why?

Very easy. Your litter box, which appeared in your cat video, is only relevant to people who have a cat right?

Do you think everyone who has watched the video, because he enjoys watching cats, also owns one?

If you would like to do that, you can do it, but you should further restrict your target audience.

For instance, you could create an ad and show it to anyone who viewed your video more than 25%, but also has an interest in "Cat Rescue". Someone who is interested in saving cats, probably also owns one or more cats.

Always try to restrict the target audience as much as possible.

In order for your ad to become viral, you should definitely create a video ad. This is very difficult with pictures, because you need for example a current and funny caricature or something similar. But that's really difficult, so I definitely recommend you to create a video.

For your video, it's not fundamentally important that it is as professional as possible. Home-made video may work even better.

However, what's important is a good picture and sound quality, which you can achieve easily with the newer smartphones on the market.

When you create a post that you want to promote later, you can either copy a link of your product into the text box, or select a product from your product catalog on Facebook (which you must have previously uploaded) to show products under your image or video with picture, price and title.

The click rates for products below a video are much better than links inside the text box.

Summary for your viral ad:

- Make sure you are among the four topics when creating it.
- Videos usually work better than pictures.
- If possible, include a small story in your video.
- Your video should not be too long - maximum 5 minutes, better 3 or even 1 minute.
- At the end, if possible, include a call to action.
- Place a link in the text and/or link the product below the video.

If you pay attention to these points, you will definitely have a better chance of creating an ad that can go viral.

Nonetheless, you do not need a viral ad to succeed with Facebook ads. Of course, it's always better if you get as much organic traffic as possible, because it costs you nothing extra, but you do not need ads that have been clicked, liked or shared millions of times.

If you get some likes and comments, that's usually enough to get a good relevance factor and get good click prices.

It's not important that your ad is going viral, but it's important that your ad matches with you, your business and your audience.

If that's the case then you can create very successful campaigns, even without a viral effect.

How much budget do I need and what can I expect?

An important point for beginners is always the budget. Apart from the fact that you want to invest as little as possible, to keep the risk low, you usually have no idea how much budget is necessary to advertise on Facebook.

In this chapter, I'll not only give you a few budget sizes along the way, but I also want to give you an outlook on what you can basically expect with your money, so you won't approach the topic with complete wrong ideas.

Minimum budget for Facebook ads

You can start placing your own ads on Facebook with 1,00 Euro per day. Of course, that's not very much, because as a rule of thumb you say that you would reach about 100 people per 1 Euro.

How many people you will reach with your ad depends very much on the interactions.

If your ad is liked, commented, or even shared by others, you'll get organic reach from your paid reach, and then you can reach over 200,000 people with your $100 budget ad.

Naturally, it is always our goal that the ad goes viral and thus becomes independent, but you cannot expect that when creating the ad.

Personally, I always test each ad set with 5 Euros. I do this for at least a week and then check the numbers. Conversion campaigns should be tested for rather two weeks, since purchases can only be made a few days after the first click on the ad.

Which key figures are important and which parameters should they have?

Please do not take this section as 100% for granted. I've been thinking for a long time whether I should even include it in this book, because those numbers that I'll provide below can really be completely different from one industry to another.

The most important thing is always that the return is higher than the investment.

Nevertheless, I just wanted to give you a few numbers on the way. As I said, the numbers can vary greatly in your industry from my numbers. It's just that you can get a rough idea for it.

Contribution interaction: 0,0001 – 0,30 Euros

Click Through Rate: 1 - 20%

Buy: 10 - 100 Euro (depending on the product !!!)

Lead: 1 - 5 euros

CPC - All: 0,05 – 0,35 Euro

CPC - Link: 0,05 – 0,50 euros

CPC - Button: 0,05 – 0,50 Euro

As I said, do not take the numbers too seriously. I just wanted to give you a rough overview. If you are in between these numbers, you are in a normal range.

Scale ads - what does that mean?

Everyone is saying that PPC is so great because it allows you to scale your ads. Apart from the fact that most people do not really manage to create scalable ads, I'd like to explain you what this word "scalable" actually means and how you can benefit from it.

When you talk about scaling an ad, that basically means raising your budget.

However, this action alone would be somewhat unrelated, because to increase the ad budget, you require some data that tells you, it could worthwhile to raise the budget.

The most important key figure is not the click through rate, the click price or anything else. The only thing that matters here is how much profit you make with this ad.

Let's take an example:

You spend 1 Euro and achieve a profit of 2 Euro. Attention, I talk here about profit, not sales!

If this works on the very small scale, 1 Euro in and 2 Euro out, then you have an ad that you can scale.

Scaling in this case means that you are now investing 10 Euros and generating 20 Euros of profit.

If that still works, then you can increase the budget, for example, to 100 Euros and make 200 Euros of profit.

You can scale it until you have exhausted your target group. So, if required you can also spend 1.000 Euros per day, if you achieve 2.000 euros of profit.

An advice at this point of time from me.

If you increase the budget, do not raise it from 5 to 500 Euros a day, because the less budget you have, the more Facebook strives to display your ad to the right people.

Sometimes, even a scaling to 100 Euros does not work anymore. Scaling directly to 500 Euros could cost you a lot of money in a short time. That's why you should always increase your ad budget step by step.

So, scaling means that you gradually increase your ad's advertising budget as soon as you've created a profitable ad and continue to increase it until it reaches a point where it's not worth it anymore.

Also, there is the possibility to reduce the advertising budget again or turn off the campaign.

Practical examples: Facebook ads

This part of the book is a bit tricky, because I really wanted to include some examples from my own experiences here, but of course I cannot hand out customer data.

However, I try to give you an insight into some of my campaigns as best as I can, without publishing names or sensitive data. I hope you understand that.

Lead: Agriculture

For a customer who is selling agriculture property, we ran a lead generation campaign.

We created a screencast video that shows the landing page that the customer arrives at when clicking the ad. There, we included a configurator for the construction and below a form with the possibility to Contact us.

We were able to create 25 offers with a supply volume of more than 700.000 Euros within a period of 4 weeks by only investing around 200 Euros in ads. That's just 8 euros per qualified lead for a product that costs 10.000 – 100.000 euros.

Direct product sales: Gold & Silver

For a customer in the gold & silver industry, I have created a direct sales campaign. As already written in the book, selling a product directly is the toughest thing to do.

Nevertheless, we have achieved a turnover of around 12,100 Euros within 4 weeks with a small budget of less than 500 Euros. The cost per customer are distributed at around 15 Euros divided per several ad sets.

It is always important to remember that we always look at the customer lifetime value and not just the first sale, even though, this was already very good. ☺

Lead: Facebook Video course

Maybe you join as well? I started a lead generation campaign. My lead magnet is a four-part course about Facebook ads. The content is really high quality and people are excited!

In 5 weeks, I generated 206 leads at just over 200 Euros, which is about one Euro per lead, which is very low.

Post interactions: Dropshipping dog toy

For a dropshipping project, I ran Page Post Engagement campaigns. A big tennis ball for Yorkshire Terriers was advertised with a video.

With only 23,93 Euro, I was able to reach 239,906 people and achieved 94,794 post interactions (Video views, Comments, Likes, Shares, etc.). The cost per post interaction was 0,0003 Euro.

I could give you many more examples, but it was important for me to give you a glimpse of my results, as there are many self-proclaimed Facebook ad experts, but few can provide really good results or even experience in the field.

Experience is one of the most important things in creating Facebook ads, and if you've developed and tested many different ads in a variety of areas, then your hit rate for a good ad will always improve over time.

The most important thing is that you start! You do not need much budget to start. Scaling and all the other stuff comes much later. Start with your first ad as soon as you can! Put this book beside you and go through everything step by step!

Believe me, it will save you a lot of hassle if you work with this book. However, if you never start, then you'll miss a good opportunity.

You will not get the same results as me from the beginning, but you will for sure get better if you stay tuned and that's what it's about.

In the next chapter, I'll show you different strategies that you can copy from me.

Ben Schneider

My strategy for lead generation

Generating Leads via Facebook ads is not difficult, but it's hard to generate leads that are as cheap as possible.

But what are cheap leads? Well, I always define that depending on reference values, but above all, on the profit that is left over at the end.

If I pay 50 Euros for a lead and 500 Euros for a sale, and at the end I have 5.000 Euros profit left, then I have no problem with these numbers.

However, if I pay 10 Euros for a lead and 100 Euros for a sale, but earn only a total of 70 Euros, then I would generate with this strategy a loss of 30 Euros and that should not be the case. (We forget about Upsells at this point of time, etc.).

First of all, a cheap lead is a lead, which basically costs you less than you earn with it.

To give you at least one number on the way, I can tell you that E-Mail leads usually move between one and ten Euros. One to five Euros per E-Mail address is the rule here.

Please do not take this number too seriously, because your industry can be much more different. I just wanted to give you an approximation, because it always annoys me when others tell you something, but you have no idea how much that actually means.

So, what do you need now to generate leads?

Of course, you need a lead magnet!

This can be a free eBook, a video course, an audiobook, an E-Mail course, free shipping or even a voucher for your online shop.

You need to give the user some reason to hand you over his email address. Nobody gives anything voluntarily and with the publication of an E-Mail address, the user gives up a piece of his anonymity on the Internet.

Actually, it is not that easy to obtain the user's E-Mail address. Your chances of receiving one, will only increase if you offer him something he desperately wants.

Put yourself in the position of your target group and think about what people really want and when they are willing to hand you their E-Mail address.

Personally, I always like to work with short video courses on a very specific topic. 3 - 4 videos of 10 - 15 minutes are completely sufficient here.

Once you've created your lead magnet, then the rest is not so hard anymore, because you already got the knowledge from me in this book.

There are two ways to run a lead campaign here. Either you choose conversion as a campaign objective, direct the people to your website and try to get the E-Mail address with an opt-in form or you directly create a lead campaign on Facebook.

The advantage of the lead campaign on Facebook is that you do not get any spam addresses, but the ones with which people are registered on Facebook. On the other hand, you

Ben Schneider

get a lot of addresses, because the process to obtain a lead is much easier for the user and more direct.

The disadvantage is, however, that you have to connect your E-Mail marketing software with a third party app, such as Zapier, for a fee, in order to include the leads automatically in your software. In addition, you are required to send a confirmation E-Mail to your Facebook-derived leads (Double Opt-In), in which they must confirm by clicking on the link in the E-Mail that you are really allowed to send messages to them.

That can sum up to additional costs of about 20 Euros per month and about 30% less registrations, since many will not confirm their E-Mail address.

Of course, that sounds quite negative right now, but I always want to tell you the whole story and do not avoid the truth.

Personally, I also work with this system, since I mostly generate my leads directly via the lead form on Facebook, because the registration rates are simply higher and, above all, the quality of the E-Mail addresses tends to be better.

To sum up, it's actually easy to generate cheap leads, you just need to give your target audience something they really want.

You can figure this out by testing what attracts users. Create multiple lead magnets and test them in different ads. Not always is the one that created most of the work, the one which works best.

My strategy to sell products directly

In this chapter, we will talk about the absolute supreme discipline in online marketing. Selling something to a customer instantly without having built trust before and without knowing us, it is really not an easy task.

You need two tools:

A perfect ad campaign on Facebook and a perfect landing page.

Although there is a lot to say about the landing page, I have to leave this topic out of the scope at this point, as this book is about Facebook ads and I could write a whole book about the topic "Selling via Landing Pages".

If you want to learn how to create highly profitable landing pages, then I can only recommend you to join my secret insider group on Facebook.

How to get there, you will find out here:

http://www.benschneider.biz/insidergruppe

So, let's focus on your ad on Facebook, which aims to sell your product/service directly to a customer.

It's not the case that it does not work. However, I seldom apply this approach to myself, as I am always following the path of trust-building tools, such as a video course.

I like to give people something, before I take something.

In my opinion, you should also make a very strong distinction as to what kind of product it is and what fundamental awareness you have with your company.

If you operate an online shop, then it is in my experience easier to directly sell products, as if you are a service provider.

But let's take a closer look at both options.

You are a service provider

You should definitely work with a video ad. With a video, you can make the user aware of your presence and make him listen to you and potentially receive a click on your ad that leads to your landing page.

Make sure that the video is not too long, but still contains some valuable information.

You should briefly tell the customer why exactly YOU are the best choice for him and who you have already helped with your service.

By doing this, you demonstrate your expert status towards the user. In addition, you should explain to him what benefits your service has and why it would be a bad decision for him, if he does not click on your landing page.

Work, as already mentioned in other chapters, with special characters and smileys. Make sure that the ad gets the attention of the user and show advantages in the text area.

Especially in the service sector, it is even harder to generate direct sales, as with an online shop, so I advise you, whether beginner or professional, that you do not lose focus if this option does not work so well for you. The alternative over the previous trust building and the retargeting approach works easier and is usually better for service providers. How this works, I'll explain in detail in the next chapter.

You run an online shop

Online shop operators have it a bit easier with direct product sales through Facebook ads.

The reason for this, is that a neat-looking online shop is usually regarded as confidence-inspiring, in comparison to a pure corporate website or a landing page.

You can sell via two options when having an online shop.

Variant 1 - You guide the customer from Facebook to the product detail page.

Variant 2 - You have previously created your own landing page and guide the user to it.

To create interest with your ad on Facebook, you can also use a video.

Usually, videos work better than pictures, whereby exceptions also confirm the rule here.

For instance, if you are creating a video of a product showing it in action, then the user can better understand the product, as if they only see a picture of it with a white background.

You have three options for your videos:

- **Product video:** Shows the product from all sides.
- **Tutorial:** You show your prospects how to use, assemble or set up the product.
- **Product in use:** You show how the product behaves in the field or what different use cases the customer

can use it for. You take away the guessing from the user.

Make sure for all videos that they are not too long. We are not on YouTube. For Facebook and especially for ads, the video should not be longer than a minute, or a maximum of two minutes, but then the video must be really exciting for the user to watch.

If you have a low view time on your ad, your relevance score will decrease. With a low relevance score (less than 7), your ad will not perform so well and cost more than you'd expect.

Video ads are very good, but it is also very important that your video is designed to be exciting, so that users from your target group watch the video as long as possible.

You can either emphasize the benefits of the product yourself in front of the camera when showing the product, or display the benefits by using text.

Always show advantages and do not focus so much on features while selling. People buy results, no features.

Benefits, as well as one or two features, can be highlighted in the text section if features are important to engage in purchasing your product.

If possible, point out in the video that the user must click on the button to get to the product.

Advertising with a product image

If you want to promote your product with just one image, please do not take the product image and just upload it to Facebook.

Show your product in action!

For example, if you sell a hat, do not show the hat with a white background, but rather a picture of a young girl laughing and wearing her hat. By doing so, you transport emotions and people buy through emotions.

You can also edit your ad image in Photoshop by, for example, showing the product from the front and back, or use a nice font for the image text.

Keep in mind that the font content must be as low as possible, otherwise you lose coverage when delivering to Facebook.

A maximum of 20% of the image should consist of fonts, and if possible, it should be even less. Still, you do not have renounce it completely.

A button in the picture with an inscription, such as "Show product" or "Click here" can help to increase the CTR (Click Through Rate) and thus increase the relevance score of your ad.

My strategy for professional Retargeting

I guess you now know that term Retargeting refers to re-addressing a person who has already come in contact with you.

To make it even more clear, I'll give you another example.

Somebody visits the "households" category in your online shop. You are now running an ad campaign on Facebook that only appears to people who visit the "households" products category on your website.

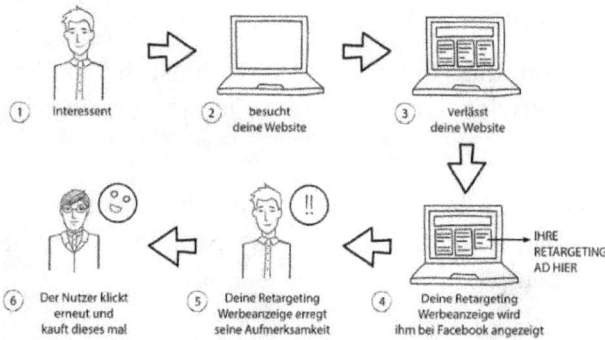

This is made possible thanks to the Facebook Pixel, which of course must be integrated on your website beforehand.

You can also create Facebook internal retargeting campaigns.

For example, anyone who liked your post or viewed your video for more than 25%.

Ben Schneider

You have some possibilities here, but it is important to me that you really understood the basics.

When does it make sense to switch to Retargeting Ads?

This strategy always makes sense if you want to convince someone who has already come in contact with your website or your product but has not bought it yet.

In short, it always makes sense, because you will never have a situation where all visitors will buy immediately.

In addition, retargeting is also useful if someone has bought a product from you and you want to sell that customer more products to increase the customer lifetime value.

Also in this case, you should run retargeting campaigns, as long as you have products that the customer has not purchased yet.

Here are some examples when you should run Retargeting Ads:

- Abandoned shopping carts
- Video Views
- Payment initiated, but not completed
- Leads
- Website visitors

Even with normal visitors of a specific category or a specific product, it may be useful to run Retargeting Ads. Most online stores generally run Retargeting ads to all website visitors.

Here are some examples that you can copy for your business.

In the following examples, I assume that you have no reach and get all your traffic through Facebook ads. Of course, you can also post on your fan page, create a YouTube video or send a newsletter to get traffic to your website.

Example for service providers

For this example, we assume that you are a consultant who wants to sell tickets for a seminar.

Most people would create an ad for the seminar tickets and try to sell them that way.

But why would anyone pay 500 Euros or more without knowing you or having been convinced by you?

I would recommend that you first write a blog post about the subject of your seminar.

Make sure that you include really valuable knowledge in the blog article, because the goal is to gain the confidence of the visitor. You need to convince the user of yourself.

Since you have installed the Facebook Pixel on your blog, you can now create a retargeting campaign on Facebook to anyone who viewed this blog post, by offering a free eBook or a free video course in exchange for their email address. Here, we are in the step of lead generation.

By the way, you can also start with the step of lead generation, but often it makes more sense for unknown experts to start off with a blog article, so the first contact is a bit gentler.

We have now launched the first retargeting campaign here. But more will follow.

You now have the customer's email address and you tagged him through the Facebook Pixel.

You should also use E-Mail marketing, but that's not the point right now.

On Facebook, you're now showing everyone who entered their E-Mail address and got your lead magnet (= free product), an ad promoting a cheap product of yours.

This could be, for example, a book, an audiobook or a video course, while this product should not be more expensive than 20 Euros.

Now comes the more exciting part.

For those who clicked on the ad, but did not end up buying your book, you are creating a retargeting campaign that shows the benefits of your book.

For those who bought your book, you create a campaign that offers another product, such as a low-cost coaching or video lesson.

Once again, you will create a retargeting campaign for those who have bought and for those who have not bought.

To anyone who has bought your last product, you are displaying an ad with your seminar. For all other users, you are again displaying an ad with the benefits of your product.

Why do we go through this process with many small steps, cheap products and retargeting campaigns?

It is quite simple. Because no one will purchase your 500 Euro seminar ticket without building trust.

You do not go on a first date and ask the woman immediately if she wants to marry you, right?

In this case it is the same principle. We first, must develop the trust so that we can turn the user into a customer.

Example for online shops

If you have an online shop, then the retargeting strategy is different, because you are dealing with other prospects / customers and other options.

With a correctly installed Facebook Pixel, we can see exactly if someone visited just one page, put something in the shopping cart, started the payment process or really bought something.

This is really important information for our retargeting campaigns.

Why?

Because through these different events we can also address the interested parties differently.

Let's start from the back to the front.

Checkout initiated, but no purchase

Someone who initiated the checkout process and then stopped, took 9 out of 10 steps. But why not the tenth?

Maybe he was worried about the payment methods or the shipping costs were too expensive or maybe he still did not have enough confidence, if our online shop is the right one for his purchase.

Now, we can run a retargeting campaign in which we show the benefits of our online store for all of those people that initiated the checkout process, but did not end up buying.

In addition, you should create another campaign, in which you simply remind the prospective customer, "Hey, you did not complete your purchase. Complete now, so we can send you your items. "

And thirdly, I would add another ad here, promoting an X% discount voucher or free shipping.

After a few days, we'll see which ad worked best, which ad people clicked on and which one did deliver the best results.

Products added to the cart, but no purchase

What could have been the problem with abandoned shopping carts? Why did they not buy?

Very often, visitors often simply put something in their shopping cart to save a product, or to see what the shipping costs will be.

Those who put something in the shopping cart are definitely interested, but are not necessarily as hot traffic as those who started the checkout process and did not complete it.

Nevertheless, retargeting campaigns pay off here enormously.

How should they look like?

Once again, we should put ourselves in the position of the interested party. What could have prevented him from going further?

Of course, confidence could be lacking. So, lets create an ad, in which we highlight the benefits of a product in our online shop. This can of course be the same ad that we have already used for the abandoned add to cart users.

In addition, I would also create an ad that comes with a voucher or free shipping.

Also, I would create an ad that leads to a blog article regarding the topic, since the customer may not be quite convinced by the product or by the topic itself.

Again, we test again and see which ad works best. If we have a clear winner, we turn off the other ads.

Retargeting website visitors

As already mentioned, the owners of online shops create Retargeting Ads to anyone who has visited the website.

You can do that either with Dynamic Ads or with normal ads, in which you display an offer, for example.

Dynamic ads have the advantage that you show the customer the product on Facebook, which he has just viewed in the online shop. He is reminded once again about the product and can directly click on the product in the ad.

To do this, you have to upload your product catalog to Facebook and then create the Retargeting Ad with your product catalog. Facebook will then automatically display the right product to the interested party in the ad.

In a normal ad, you could highlight a special offer from your online shop. However, this only makes sense if you have specialized in a certain niche with your online shop. If you own an online shop that offers underwear and cordless screwdrivers, then this kind of advertising makes no sense.

However, you could still run retargeting ads to visitors of individual categories. This gives you the opportunity to show all underwear customers a special underwear offer and to the customers who are interested in cordless screwdriver, an offer for a pair of cordless screwdrivers.

You can do that also for Dynamic Retargeting Ads. In this way, you show the prospective the product, which he has looked at, and on the other hand you show him a special offer in your online shop.

This can work very well in combination.

Test, test, test!

Until this stage, you have learned everything in this book that you need to know about Facebook ads. Theoretically, you now have the knowledge to run ads like the pros.

Unfortunately, I must tell you that even experts do not just turn on ads that go through the roof.

Sure, our results are certainly better than the ones for beginners and yes, our ads are designed based on knowledge and experience in order to go through the roof, but nevertheless I am always honest with my community and my customers and the truth is that we still have to test.

Of course, there are ads that go right through the ceiling. Nonetheless, this chapter is a very important one for you.

If you create ads on Facebook, then you should always create several. Try different pictures and videos. Try different campaign objectives and ad sets. Every target group reacts differently, but you cannot know in advance how well it will react to which image or video.

Not only can you test different pictures, videos and audiences, you can also test different offers.

Maybe a product for 19,90 Euros will receive much more clicks than a product which is worth 9,90 Euros. You won't be able to know until you have tested it.

Always make sure that you do not stop your tests too soon. My strategy is always to test for 5 Euros at least for 7 days. I check the ads every day, but do not touch them after seven days at the earliest.

The ads may take some time to settle and it can be the case that you will get after six days better results than after two days.

In addition, you should look at conversion campaigns, if and how many sales were generated.

The best numbers will not help you, if the sales are missing.

For conversion campaigns, you can set the conversion window. I always use 7 days after clicking. This makes perfect sense in e-commerce, since many buyers only decide to buy after several approaches.

If you have now set seven days but shut down the campaign after seven days, then you would have tracked only those who bought either immediately, or at least within those seven days.

That's why you can turn off conversion campaigns after seven days if no sales were made, but you should still watch them for a week.

If you realize that there have been sales, you put the ads with the sales, back to active.

It is always important for your analysis that an ad is worthwhile. It does not matter if the lead costs you one or 20 Euros. The only important thing is whether you make profit or loss.

To reach the best outcome, it is important that you test your ads! Create even 20 ads for the same purpose if you want to.

You have no limit on Facebook. The important thing is to find an ad that works so well that you can increase your budget and scale the ad.

That's why the motto of Facebook ads after creation is always: Testing, testing, testing! ☺

Why advertising on Facebook is only half the story

The book is coming to an end and you've read a lot about Facebook ads and also about marketing and sales approaches from me.

What we have not talked about in detail, though, is that Facebook ads alone are not enough.

Everything you read in the pages of this book is very important to your business, but it's only half the story.

The other half concerns your website/online shop/landing page.

Your ads may be great, but if your landing pages or sites behind them are not, you can have a problem.

If you want to generate leads and your prospect can not find an opt-in form, then you can have the best ad in the world, but you won't get any leads.

If possible, you should always use a landing page to redirect you from Facebook ads.

Never guide people in e-commerce to the home page of your online store. That does not work. The visitors will leave again, because they do not want to search for anything in your online shop.

Make sure that you are always targeting ads to an action or product, and that the landing page behind is designed for just one action or product.

Anything that could distract the visitor from your destination should not stand in the way. Especially in the online shop, it is often difficult to keep the visitor's attention as the menu can be quite dense and users quickly click away.

An ad and a landing page serve only one purpose and nothing else is allowed in here. Both are about a product or a service and not two, three or more things. Simply a single one!

If you want to learn how online marketing works holistically profitable, then I can only recommend you to join my secret insider group on Facebook.

How to get to my insider group, you can find out here: http://www.benschneider.biz/insidergruppe

Conclusion

I really hope that you understood everything from this book, so could expand your knowledge on Facebook ads.

I can only impart theoretical knowledge to you via these pages. In practice, you must do it yourself in the end.

The important thing is that you spend your time on your ads and really think deeply. Do not start with too much budget and do not start with wrong expectations.

Anyone can create ads on Facebook these days, but there's a reason why there are professionals who only dedicate their time to this topic/profession.

It is important to me that you come into action and I have personally made you smarter with this book.

Start thinking about your first or next ad today. Start with the implementation today!

I have used more than 10.000 Euros in budget, ran hundreds of ads, and gained years of experience to obtain the knowledge and experience I conveyed to you in this book.

It does not all happen overnight, but if you have a jump-start, like this book, then you can have huge success with Facebook ads in a very short time.

Unfortunately, I did not have this jump start back then, but you have it! You hold this book in your hands! You know my YouTube Channel and have the opportunity to contact me and join my secret insider group on Facebook.

You have the opportunity to get help, so take advantage of it because it will not only save you time, but also money!

I would be glad if you would write a review on Amazon about this book. This will help me to reach my goal of becoming a bestseller on Amazon. This is not just a saying, but you would really help me a lot.

Just go to the product page of this book on Amazon and leave your opinion at the bottom of the page. I read all the reviews myself and would be very happy to read one of yours.

If you still have questions about Facebook ads, feel free to contact me via the contact form on my website.

I wish you all the best from the bottom of my heart and good luck with your ads on Facebook.

Catapult your business to the next level!

Your Ben

My offer for you!

I want you to get started! That's why I cordially invite you to my insider group and would like to reward you twice for buying this book!

With the coupon code **"FBBuch"** or under the following link,

http://www.benschneider.biz/insidergruppe2018-FBBUCH

you save 10€ for your access to my Facebook insider group!

Reading and acquiring the knowledge is one thing. Implementing the knowledge learned, continuing to train on a weekly basis and asking me your personal questions is another thing and that is exactly what will make your sales figures explode!

Take this opportunity!

Ben Schneider

Notes

Notes

Ben Schneider

www.ingramcontent.com/pod-product-compliance
Lightning Source LLC
Chambersburg PA
CBHW050509210326
41521CB00011B/2389